BREAD IN THE DESERT

Bread in the Desert

by
Pierre Talec

Translated by
Edmond Bonin

NEWMAN PRESS
New York / Paramus / Toronto

A Newman Press edition, originally published under the title
Un grand desir by Le Centurion/Le Cerf, Paris, France, © 1971.

Copyright © 1973 by
The Missionary Society
of St. Paul the Apostle
in the State of New York

Library of Congress
Catalog Card Number: 72-95650

ISBN 0-8091-0178-5 (cloth)
ISBN 0-8091-1763-0 (paper)

Published by Newman Press
Editorial Office: 1865 Broadway, N.Y., N.Y. 10023
Business Office: 400 Sette Drive, Paramus, N.J. 07652

Printed and bound in the
United States of America

Contents

Preface

Prayer may be viewed as the most natural and spontaneous, the easiest and simplest of human attitudes—or just the opposite. Quite instinctively, we feel the necessity of turning to God, especially in certain situations. To express ourselves and be understood by him, we need not use high-flown language or worry lest our ineloquence thwart our purpose. But the one we speak to is not there before us. We hear no answer to our cries, nor can we see the reactions of him whose presence we take on faith alone. Under the circumstances, how can prayer be defined as a dialogue with God? Is it not rather a soliloquy by the soul?

Yet Scripture constantly asserts that, unlike idols, God speaks; and we acknowledge Christ as God's Word made flesh.

Moreover, the Church, following Israel, has from the start always been a community which regularly gathers its members for communal celebrations of prayer and the liturgy. Private prayer, the soliloquy of the soul addressing God without words, cannot suffice either believers or the Church.

Since God speaks, we must begin by listening to him. Since his words ring out in the assembly, we must begin by coming together to hear them. Then prayer can spring forth, conveying the individual and group response of the faithful. If we speak, it is always in reply to God, who spoke first. Consequently, prayer rightly fits into the framework of a dialogue.

But this dialogue is an ongoing process. Only little by little do we grasp the meaning, the scope and the consequences of what God says:

1

indeed, we shall never comprehend it fully. However, ours is not merely the task of ever more deeply scrutinizing the objective significance, so to speak, of a conception which would possess all its value in and for itself.

God's message is directed to me—this day—and to the community which I constitute along with my brothers in the faith. To both of us it reveals what I am and what we are together. Our response today is not the final word, for each individual and community is confronted anew every time by God's voice ceaselessly summoning us to reply. This is the dialogue of prayer and its demanding dialectic.

Father Talec's prayers command attention first of all precisely because they are situated at this level and in this perspective. Their inner dynamism, their development, could be summed up in the following pattern: "We have heard, Lord. You say . . . Yes, but today we . . . So . . ." As circumstances dictate, these terms can be transposed without changing anything, for we may also come before God to tell him immediately about ourselves, our plans, our problems, our confusion, our inability to understand—in a word, our whole life. To whom could we reveal all this if not to him? On one condition, however: that we pause to let ourselves be probed, challenged and called to order by God's word, till finally the dialogue reaches this zenith of communion: a genuine *Amen* witnessing to both his fidelity and our fidelity to him.

Such prayer could nevertheless remain highly individual. That is not what Father Talec had in mind when composing the prayers published here. They were written in a specific community [Saint-Séverin], for it and, I might even say, with it. Not that they are the product of a team or a board: the creative collaboration I am alluding to is of a different order and far more profound.

Speaking in the midst of one's brothers in order to voice their prayer before God, requires oneness of life with them, keen attention to what they are experiencing, and antennas to sense it. Then the community can recognize these prayers as its own and see that it has collaborated actively and vitally in creating them, though only one man has put them into words.

At the same time, they achieve the authentic concreteness expected of them. It does not result from amassing details that pertain more to information and so often lapse into anecdotage —something which has no place here. Rather, one becomes genuinely concrete when, in his own flesh, he profoundly perceives the meaning, the import, the beauty or the tragedy of the life his brothers are living, however dull and commonplace it may seem to a casual observer.

When this is expressed in a way that makes us transcend its individuality, concrete prayer acquires a certain universal character, at least for the greater part of the congregation.

Though produced in a particular community, the prayers in *Bread in the Desert* may prove useful to many another, concerned, not with the specific situations which they presuppose, but with the endeavor which they echo and which other situations invite us to make likewise.

Thus, two dangers forever threaten: a disembodied prayer which has no roots anywhere on earth, and a certain type of "relevant" prayer which is so particularized that it has meaning only for an individual or a group to the exclusion of everyone else. Father Talec successfully avoids both pitfalls in these prayers, which nonetheless remain very concrete.

Their adaptability derives from yet another

feature—their style. When sentences are rigidly framed and every word in them is strictly defined to carry a single meaning, so that nothing can be changed without destroying them, they possess perfect clarity and smooth-flowing harmony. Prayers thus phrased mark out a sharply defined path with no unexpected turns ahead; but they present no opportunity to pause, either: once we have set foot on this carefully posted road, we must move along without exploring the byways. Spiritual freedom may very likely feel uncomfortable on it. Such prayer, though perhaps perfect in itself, does not necessarily correspond to everyone's needs and potential. How can we manage to reconcile the personal and the communal character of public prayer? How can we help the individual to enter personally into a group exercise?

I believe the prayers presented here answer this purpose. Often the sentences are deliberately left unfinished, without a period to close them. Consequently, they afford us the possibility of pursuing an idea as the Spirit bids, and even in directions which no one could foresee and which we ourselves may not have anticipated while planning our itinerary. Then prayer becomes an invitation or a provocation to prayer.

No verbalization can be neutral; it necessarily bears the stamp of a particular subjectivity. But when an author speaks the language of poetry, when he evokes more than he affirms, when he suggests without imposing, his personal commitment does not become an intolerable coercion. He succeeds in drawing us from our own neutrality, without letting us escape into some vaguely "religious" emotion elicited by a beautiful text which we do not really assimilate. Father Talec has finally agreed to publish these prayers because the congregation at Saint-

Séverin often requested the text of them and persuaded him they would prove helpful to others also for the various celebrations as well as for private prayer. Even if they only inspired further compositions, they would still be useful.

As will be obvious, the vocabulary of these prayers makes very discreet use of certain classical terms that are rich in meaning, provided we grasp their full import. The fact is, however, that many of them now convey notions which, to say the least, hardly square with their authentic denotation—that of tradition and sound theology. For example, the word *grace* designates that attitude which characterizes God alone and translates his love for those to whom he gratuitously grants salvation. To many of us, does it not immediately suggest purely external help from above to perform acts—possibly of the moral order—which would otherwise be too difficult or even impossible? And that is half bad. For we also beg God for the "grace" to pass exams, not to have an accident, and so forth. Such requests are certainly legitimate, but meanwhile the word *grace* takes on a whole gamut of meanings blurred by ambiguities. We could adduce many other examples, not for the purpose of systematically striking from the vocabulary of prayer all words which are subject to some equivocation, but, rather, in the hope that abstaining from them temporarily may lead to rediscovering them in the fulness of their significance. Then we shall be able to use them anew to express what both we and they mean. Accordingly, there is no question here of obstinate bias but, on the contrary, of pedagogical intent which enhances the value of these prayers further still.

In addition, they bespeak an evident catechetical concern, without, for all that, falling into the typically ecclesiastical foible of turning everything into a sermon. Prayer is a request to God for something; but it is also a step toward him, a beginning of conversion, or a deepening of our relationship with him. This has to be expressed somehow. In public worship, moreover, prayer cannot content itself with stating what we already are; since it is everyone's prayer, at what "average" level should it remain? Uttered by the priest, it must also, especially after the proclamation of God's word, help us to rise higher: it is not merely "declarative" but "optative," so to speak. Thus, it expresses not only our faith, hope and charity, but also what we desire to be and intend to do in order to attain that goal in our everyday living.

Lastly—and this is not the least of their merits —the prayers collected in this volume are almost always related, in one way or another, to the Eucharist and the celebration of it. Indeed, can we conceive of Christian prayer which would not be Eucharistic, which would not explicitly or implicitly tie in with Christ's "priestly prayer," and not rely on his promise that the Father will hear and answer us? Must not all Christian prayer look toward the Lord's Supper or flow from it? As Saint Paul reminds us, the life we bring and express in prayer constitutes our spiritual offering to God; now, we cannot make this offering unless we unite it with the perfect sacrifice which was offered to the Father once and for all, and which the Eucharist actualizes sacramentally.

The preceding thoughts were suggested by a reading of Father Talec's prayers which I am happy to introduce to a wider public.

The variety of texts will help to make this collection useful and timely. Greetings or "invitations," as it were, merely indicate a theme or suggest an attitude: they are like runways from which prayer may freely take flight. Litanic prayers, often the merest outlines, will permit the celebrant to work out a more structured prayer as circumstances require. Other texts, on the contrary, are more fully developed than those in the Missal but, as I remarked earlier, do not imprison prayer within their limits. All in all, this volume provides material for various celebrations and for private prayer.

I now wish to thank Father Talec for agreeing to this publication and kindly asking me to write the preface to it.

Robert Gantoy

Our God

How Beautiful
Is Our God!

Morning sun, evening sun,
gliding over the waters,
light bathing in the waves,
beautiful beyond words . . .
God, our Father, immerse us
in your beauty!

Fire of God, fire over the earth,
enkindling in our hearts . . .
Christ Jesus, we want to live,
to live with soul aflame!

Storm wind, gusty wind,
folly of God at the center of our lives . . .
Spirit, come from every corner
of the world,
breathe, and let the storm break forth!

• Litanic prayer at the Kyrie on Trinity Sunday.

Triune God,
over and over we say
that you are great, supreme, infinite;
we proclaim your glory;
we speak to you of grace . . .
But who shall speak of your beauty?
Who can contemplate it?

You are beautiful, O Lord!
This is your feast . . .
Let us tell you of your beauty
till the day we can gaze on you
face to face
in the silence of eternity,
for ever and ever.

● Opening prayer on Trinity Sunday.

12

God Here Below,
God Far Away

Just as a sailor
watches for the coast
and thinks he sees a beacon ahead,
so do our eyes scan the horizon of God.
But he has ascended into heaven . . .

• Greeting on the solemnity of the Ascension.

Lord, you have gone away.
You came and will come back again.
For your love is everlasting.

You draw us, and you pass unnoticed;
made manifest, you remain hidden . . .
God here below, God far away . . .
For your love is everlasting.

Your presence is imperceptible . . .
We seek your will
on earth as in heaven.
For your love is everlasting.

• Litanic prayer at the Kyrie on the solemnity of the
Ascension.

Lord,
what would your eternity be
if heaven above
consisted only in forgetting
this earth here below?

Do not look down on us!
We aspire to live as of today
what we shall live tomorrow,
for ever and ever.

● Opening prayer on the solemnity of the Ascension.

Lord,
how high have you been lifted up?
Is not the summit of your glory
also the summit of your love?
You take us up in that love,
and our life becomes your Ascension.
What could be more thrilling!

But who can ever measure up
to your love?
Teach us to take one more step
each day,
and the infinity of your love
will appear more real to us
than the confines of our sadness.
Then your promise will come true:
that no one can take your joy from us,
since it is already the joy
of all eternity.

● Prayer at the General Intercessions on the solemnity of
  the Ascension.

Lord,
may this Eucharist be,
at the heart of our lives,
a patient ascension
in your love,
day by day
for ever and ever.

• Prayer after communion on the solemnity of the
  Ascension.

Lord Jesus,
in proclaiming that you
were lifted up to heaven
and sit at the right hand of the Father,
we docilely repeat
what you have chosen to reveal to us.

We give you thanks
for speaking to us as you see fit.

But what do these representations
of your glory mean?
Would you, the eternal God,
be the God of some other age?

Grant that the people of today
may be able to receive your word
as the news of all ages.

• Another opening prayer on the Sunday after the solemnity of the Ascension.

Truly, Father most holy,
you, the God beyond all space,
we lift up our hearts
on this day
when we celebrate the Ascension
of Jesus Christ, our Lord.

Through faith in this mystery
we are invited
to seek the light of your kingdom,
that kingdom without clouds.
And we are called
to live as if each of us
saw the invisible,
on earth as in heaven.

That is why,
searching for the signs
of your presence here below
and hoping to attain the goods above,
we raise our song of joy to you
and say with a single voice:
Holy, holy, holy . . .

• Preface on the solemnity of the Ascension.

Lord Jesus,
as we try to draw near to you,
do not pretend you are far away;
do not move off, like a mirage.

Let our gaze grow accustomed
to seeing you
just as you appear:
always through signs
but always, too, beyond appearances—
you who are life beyond death
for ever and ever!
Amen.

- Opening prayer on the Sunday when the gospel about
  the disciples from Emmaus (Luke 24, 13-35) is proclaimed.

The Power
and the Glory

"Glory to God
in highest heaven."
Lord God, Father almighty,
your glory is immense,
for your only might is that of love.
We give you thanks
for being able to glorify you.
Does not your glory, Lord, consist
in receiving from men
this love which you give them?
We praise you, we bless and adore you.

Lord Jesus Christ,
only Son of the Father,
you came upon earth
to sing his glory.
You were never glorious among men,
but you will be fully glorified
when peace reigns throughout the world
for all those whom you love!
As we await that day,
we praise you, we bless and adore you.

Spirit of God,
with the Father and the Son,
you are the Most High.
We want to believe
that "all the sufferings of the present
are nothing
compared to the glory to come."
But at the same time, we have to admit
that "our hope for that great day
is not sufficient
to nourish our human hopes
from day to day."
In this expectation,
we praise you, we bless and adore you.

• Prayer of thanksgiving for possible use as a hymn on
the theme of "Glory to God."

Lord Jesus,
it is over:
the heavens no longer open up;
gone is the dove—and the angels, too.
The age of wonders is closed.
And yet,
what could be more astounding:
at every Eucharist
we share in the power of your love!

When we present
the heavy bread of our weakness,
may we show
that your glory is not in prodigies
but in the hidden faithfulness
which remains
a loving presence
hour by hour,
for ever and ever.

• Prayer at the General Intercessions during the season of Epiphany when the gospel concerning Jesus' baptism (Matthew 3, 13-17) is proclaimed.

Lord Jesus,
while awaiting that "hour"
when your glory will be revealed,
grant to all who languish
in their dull daily routine
the desire to live
according to your love.

In this Eucharist,
the superexcellent sign
of all transformations,
may this bread and wine,
having become your body and your life,
nourish our hope
as we await eternity.

● Prayer after communion during the season of Epiphany
when the gospel about the miracle at Cana (John 2, 1-2)
is proclaimed.

24

The Kingdom

Brothers and sisters,
we proclaim that Christ is King
and say aloud
what Jesus himself reveals to us:
"My kingdom is not of this world."

God's world—man's world:
our world . . .
our kingdom . . .

• Greeting on the solemnity of Christ the King (John 18, 33-38).

Our Father, you are in heaven
as on earth . . .
Earth!
The universe of Jesus Christ . . .
your kingdom!

> *Glory to you throughout the ages.*

Lord Jesus,
your kingdom is not of this world.
O wonder!
We who are in this world
belong to your kingdom.

> *Glory to you throughout the ages.*

Holy Spirit,
you dwell in our hearts . . .
What grandeur!
Each of us is your kingdom.

> *Glory to you throughout the ages.*

• Litanic prayer at the Kyrie on the solemnity of Christ
the King (John 18, 33-38).

Lord Jesus,
only the pure in heart can see,
through the shadows
of the petty kingdoms we construct,
the radiance of your great kingdom.

Let your sunlight enter into us . . .
Grant us the transparence
of single-minded men,
and someday we shall see things right.

You give your kingdom
to the poor in spirit,
as you have said,
for ever and ever.

● Opening prayer on the solemnity of Christ the King
(John 18, 33-38).

Lord Jesus,
"you are a king, then?"
You claimed no title,
but only told Pilate,
"It is you who say I am a king.
I was born and came into the world
to bear witness to the truth,
and everyone who loves the truth
listens to my voice."

May your kingdom come
now and for ever!

- Prayer at the General Intercessions on the solemnity of
  Christ the King (John 18, 33-38).

28

Invisible God,
You Are the Spirit

We give you thanks,
Father of all beginnings . . .
How many stars have shone,
how many days have dawned
since that eternal morning
when earth first awoke
in the enthusiasm of the Spirit!

Since always, you are life,
O Holy Spirit!
For ages,
we human beings had possessed life,
but what did we know about your life
in ours?
Now you have given your name
to everything we call
ardor, daring, wisdom,
fire, passion, love . . .

Just as the earth crackles
after the hard freeze of winter,
how could our joy not break out now
with a single voice:
Holy, holy, holy is the Lord . . .

• Preface during the season of Pentecost.

HYMN TO THE HOLY SPIRIT

Spirit of God,
breath of life,
you are, at the heart of our lives,
the air of God which we inhale.

Spirit of God,
light of life,
you are, at the heart of our lives,
the joy to which we aspire.

Spirit of God,
source of life,
you are, at the heart of our lives,
the "divine milieu"
which we sense all around us.

Creator Spirit,
youth of our hearts,
you inspire every prayer
we address to the Father.

Spirit of truth,
unfailing brightness,
your radiance does not blind us
but is our light.

Spirit of strength,
you are almighty,
with a might that never compels:
the power of your love giving itself.

30

Spirit of love,
you are the Spirit of the risen Jesus.
At Pentecost, you manifested yourself.
Pentecost is every day,
for ever and ever:
your love.

Spirit of unity,
you give us your unity
as Christ leaves us his peace.
Do not look only upon our divisions
but upon the faith of the baptized . . .

● Meditation hymn (sequence) on Pentecost Sunday.

God, you are the Spirit!
What would our life be
without your life?
How could we speak of light
without your light?
How discover joy
without your joy?

Inexpressible presence,
unfathomable truth,
you show us what you are:
freedom!
In it,
you call us to love
for ever and ever!

In this Eucharist, O Lord,
we give you thanks
for the vitality of your Spirit,
the discretion of his presence,
the freedom which he leaves us
and the trust he has placed in us
for ages and ages.

God of Tenderness,
You Are the Father

Lord, there are so many things
we cannot express!
Your tenderness is insight
into what goes unsaid,
and makes every word ring out
in perfect pitch with love.

Lord, there are so many things
which cannot be put into words.
Your tenderness
is the silent longing of love.
You let us guess . . .

Lord, there is so much living to do!
Your tenderness
is the genius of your love,
always ready to improvise.

● Litanic prayer at the Kyrie on a Sunday during Eastertide when John's gospel on the love of the Father (John
16, 27-28) is proclaimed.

Like a breeze,
O Lord,
your tenderness is imperceptible.
Like an ocean wind,
the force of your love is irresistible.

But you draw
only those who want to follow you;
you allure
only those who let themselves be loved.

From the bottom of our heart
—or at least our lips—
we say, as best we can,
"I love you."

● Opening prayer on a Sunday during Eastertide when John's gospel on the love of the Father (John 16, 27-28) is proclaimed.

Lord Jesus,
whenever we celebrate the Eucharist
in memory of you,
your words come alive:
"If anyone loves me, I shall love him."

Take over our lives,
so that they may manifest
the life you share
with the Father and the Spirit,
God of tenderness
for all eternity!

● Prayer after communion on a Sunday during Eastertide when John's gospel on the love of the Father (John
16, 27-28) is proclaimed.

Only Son of God, We Are Proud of You

Lord Jesus,
like children
who have no title
to offer congratulations
but voice their admiration all the louder,
we proclaim
that we are proud of you,
for you are the only true Son.
You lived and died
so that we might live.
You are life, our life;
God, our God;
alone with the Father and the Spirit
for ever and ever.

- Opening prayer on a Sunday during Christmastide when
the prologue to John's gospel (John 1, 1-18) is
proclaimed.

Lord Jesus,
broaden the boundaries of our hearts.
We would so want to make you proud
of having given us everything—
including your very self!

That is your glory—
you, the only Son,
together with the Father and the Spirit
for ever and ever.

• Prayer after communion on a Sunday during Christmastide when the prologue to John's gospel (John 1, 1-18)
is proclaimed.

Christ Jesus, One of Us

"The Firstborn
of All Creation..."

PRELUDE TO CHRISTMAS:
"HE BECAME MAN..."

Christ Jesus—
a man in our midst.
But what a man:
the only Son of God,
the only child of a carpenter,
Mary's and Joseph's little boy.

You knew the things we know,
and you realize
you did not know everything.
In your infinite knowledge,
you know all things
and see that everything has limitations.
In your universal experience,
you know everything;
but you once felt the limitations
of human knowledge.
You could not be everything
or do everything
at the same time:
you could not be both dark and fair,
both an Easterner and a Westerner,
a Jew and an Arab,
a rustic and a townsman,
an only child and one of many,
a celibate and a married man,
a craftsman and an intellectual;
you could not be both healthy and sickly;
you could not die in the prime of life
and still taste old age.

And yet you knew a great deal
about the details of everyday living:
like the yeast in the dough,
from watching your Mother bake bread;
or lost coins,
from seeing the lady next door panic
and turn her house inside out
till she found her silver piece.
And you knew plenty
about men and women and children:
about Peter and Judas,
about Mary, your Mother,
and the other Mary—Magdalene,
about the Samaritan woman
with her five husbands,
the woman with none,
and those little rascals playing funeral
and tooting on flutes.

And how you loved life!
Nobody stays in the mountains,
alone for hours,
unless he is something of a poet . . .
Your hands caressed the wild flowers
no one ever picks;
you saw those forgotten olive groves;
and the withered fig trees inspired you,
like the birds of the air
that say sweet nothings
as they stutter for joy,
like the lilies of the field
that trust to heaven,
like the endlessly rolling desert
and the everlastingly beautiful sea.
You contemplated the Mediterranean
and the little Sea of Galilee,
its blue waters studded with whitecaps,
reflecting the pale clouds
that raced above,

or churned up by a storm from Tiberias,
with squally winds, frantic flowers,
bristling blades of grass
and people crazed with fear.

People—you know us well . . .
You know what we know,
what we are worth
and what we love.
You know that we love
and that we do not know how to love.
And if there is one thing you know
better than anyone else,
it is what we call "love,"
though it may not always be
what you love—
you who are Love itself.

CHRISTMAS PRAYER

God whom we call Jesus,
you chose to dwell among us.
How wonderful when we think of it!
Mankind had been expecting you;
but even so, on the part of a God,
this is most unexpected.
During your life as a man,
you wanted to be like us
and act like us.
Everything could have begun so well;
but, from the first,
you took chances.
You already had your ideas
about the beatitudes.
So the beginnings were difficult.
Still, we must not exaggerate:
many another, before you,
suffered hardship from the start.
You had no luck in Bethlehem,
no lodgings.
Hotels are always like that.
Mary and Joseph
should have arrived sooner.
But the fact is that you had Egypt,
together with everything the gospels say
and everything they do not say,
and it all worked out well.

For a good number of years
you led a cozy, quiet life
in your home at Nazareth.
You lived like a son, a real one;
like a friend, accessible to all—
which did not save you
from having enemies.
And within a very short period,

44

you said and did a great many things
and saw large numbers of people.
Your friends
—Mary, Martha and Lazarus—
welcomed you at Bethany.
From Cana to Emmaus,
you received invitations.
You ate at Simon's,
and God knows how the neighbors gossiped;
you stopped over at Zacchaeus' house,
and again people talked.
As a result of all this,
you died on the cross.

But you are risen.
And now
your dwelling is vast like the world,
universal in your Church,
interior in our hearts.
Both here and there,
always at home,
for ever and ever,
you are with us, Emmanuel.

Christmas! Christmas is here!
Cries of joy in the night:
"A child has been born for us,
a son given to us."
It is done:
Jesus Christ, the Son of God,
has become man,
the savior of all men.
Let us acclaim Emmanuel,
for today is Christmas!
Christmas! Christmas is here!

● Greeting at a Mass on Christmas.

For ages and ages,
O God, our God,
the winds have been blowing
and buffeting the world.
What a wretched little thing
is this poor world of ours . . .

For ages and ages,
O God, our God,
the seas have been rising
and falling with the tides.
What bitterness boils up
in these poor hearts of ours . . .

For ages and ages,
O God, our God,
the stars have been remembering heaven:
so there is always a speck of joy
in the atmosphere.

• Hymn or litanic prayer at the Kyrie of a Mass on
Christmas.

Lord Jesus,
for eternities now,
heaven and earth,
like fond grandparents,
have thrilled at the sight
of the children's children
ever bringing forth children . . .

And now,
amid the starlit night,
comes the incomparable Child,
the smile of God
and tenderness toward mankind.

We beg you, Lord,
revive in us
the joy of your joy
for ever and ever.

Lord Jesus,
you have come to live among us.
What do you think of us now?
Are you sorry you came?

Do not go away;
but be patient with us,
for you are one of us—
the one who saves.
Flesh of our flesh,
save our joy!

● Prayer at the General Intercessions of a Mass on
Christmas.

Lord Jesus,
you grew,
grew tremendously on the cross . . .
You have wondrously exalted us
by your resurrection . . .
And now in this communion
your greatness becomes ours.

Thanks for this Christmas Eucharist
which we partake of
with the joy of children . . .
May it give birth,
in the depths of our hearts,
to an ever-increasing desire
to live like children of God,
starting today,
in this joy from the kingdom
promised to the "little ones,"
for ever and ever.

• Prayer after communion at a Mass on Christmas.

How good it is
to let night overtake us
when that night is Light itself!
How pleasant to render thanks
as we celebrate Jesus' birth!

Christ Jesus!
How beautiful your name is on this night,
like a star in our darkness . . .

Christ Jesus!
You stand alone:
the Son, the Son of God, God from God,
sent by the Father,
conceived by the Spirit,
Word made flesh,
born of a woman, the Virgin Mother—
Mary, beautiful beyond all other women.

Christ Jesus!
You are universal:
the Brother, the Brother of mankind,
marvelously human,
a miracle of love.

Let all creation clap its hands
and flap its wings
and spread the blessed news;
and from Venus to Mars,
let all the stars and planets repeat:
"Emmanuel has come to live on earth!"
Let the light shine bright
in every home;

let gladness shout
from every rooftop;
and hope sing out
as with one voice:
Holy, holy, holy . . .

● Preface for Christmas.

Lord Jesus,
you were tiny, very tiny in Bethlehem—
the most adorable of newborn babes.
And then you grew up,
without ever losing any of the beauty
of children who smile.
Teach us to grow up
and rediscover that smile . . .

> *Enlighten our hearts, O Lord.*

Lord Jesus,
you were cold, very cold in Bethlehem.
But your love
has warmed the whole world!
Oh, on this Christmas night,
how we would like you to find
in our hearts
the warmth of your own love!

> *Enlighten our hearts, O Lord.*

Lord Jesus,
your Mother showed
great tenderness in Bethlehem,
and Joseph was like a real father to you,
thinking of everything . . .
Help us, on this Christmas night,
to bring a ray of joy
to those you have chosen
as our father and mother on earth . . .

> *Enlighten our hearts, O Lord.*

• Litanic prayer at the Kyrie for a children's Mass on Christmas.

Lord Jesus,
what a lot of people
there were at the crib:
Mary, Joseph,
the shepherds with their sheep,
and all those angels in the sky—
it must have been extraordinary!
And then all who are not mentioned:
cousin Elizabeth, perhaps,
and John the Baptist—why not?

We do not really know
exactly who was in Bethlehem that night,
under the stars.
But what we do know
is that you did not forget anyone:
you came for all the children
and all the men and women
of all times and places.

So today we want to make room—
a lot of room—
in our hearts
for everyone you love.
May all those who are looking for you
with the simplicity of a child's heart
find you now,
for a feast
that will last for ever and ever.
Amen.

• Opening prayer at a children's Mass on Christmas.

"In Him Is All Perfection..."

GENERAL INTERCESSIONS
ON GOOD FRIDAY

For the Church

Spirit of truth,
we pray to you
for the Church you animate,
the Church of Jesus Christ,
our Church . . .

In good days
as well as bad,
teach us to recognize
in your beloved Church
the "eternal companion"
Christ has chosen for himself
in order to present her to us
as one presents one's mother . . .
since it is in her
that we live with you
for ever and ever.

Also for the Church

Lord Jesus,
we pray for your Church so often
that our prayers become mere words,
a constant harping on the same string.

We are moved to pity
over your physical body
because it tasted death.
But how about your Church,
your body living today?

Forgive us for mutilating,
by our criticism,
your body which is the Church.

Forgive us for disfiguring,
by our sins,
your body which is the Church.

Make us love your Church,
and you will be able to show her forth
as you already see her—
without stain or wrinkle
or anything of the sort,
but faultless and holy.

For the Pope

Lord Jesus,
to this man whom the Church
has chosen as her shepherd,
grant
firmness of belief,
boldness to seek,
and light to lead.

And for himself personally,
in his life as a man,
may he find a bit of peace,
serenity in the midst of trials
and joy in friendship,
from day to day,
as he awaits the life to come.

For Bishops and Priests

Lord Jesus,
you know that priests would want
to be more available
to the people of these times.

In their desire
to make their priesthood a service,
they try to lend an ear
to everyone who comes along.
But what contradictory cries they hear!

To these men whom you have chosen
to gather communities together
grant patience, serenity
and—why not?—
a bit of a sense of humor . . .

Help our bishops find
in brotherly cooperation
the assurance they need
to take the risks required
by a Church that is moving forward.

Do not forget our own bishop,
for whom we pray with affection.
Despite his office,
he is still a man . . .
Make him find
the confidence he inspires,
the warmth he spreads
and the simplicity he reflects,
so that all of us together
may offer an example of love
here and now and for ever.

For Chiefs of State

Lord Jesus,
for centuries earth has trembled
with fear of fratricidal wars,
and by now we are tired
of begging you for impossible peace . . .

And yet you remain our surest hope:
we can look to the cross as a promise,
and your resurrection
holds out certitude.

But our faith wavers
before the crises men create.
What is the use of asking you
to lead chiefs of state
according to your Spirit of justice,
if the nations themselves
do not walk in brotherhood?
For all who guide and govern
the destiny of countries,
we pray to you,
unable to add anything further
or be more specific . . .

For Those Preparing for Baptism

Lord Jesus,
during these Paschal celebrations
we renew the marvel of our baptism
years ago.

Look with tenderness
upon those now preparing for baptism
and, in the freshness of their faith,
discovering the Church
as she is.

Help us not to disappoint them.
May they find genuine communities
so that,
in their persistent quest,
with heart unclouded,
they may give you thanks
today and every day,
now and for ever.

For All Who Are Suffering

Lord Jesus,
could anyone but you,
who carried the cross to Calvary,
maintain that life's burden is light?

To all who are crushed,
and all who tend to live frivolously,
grant the strength of your love,
and make us attentive
to all who suffer
on their own way of the cross:
the sick,
the prisoners,
the refugees,
the lonely,
the unloved,
the despised,
the misunderstood . . .
Teach us to discover your cross
in our crosses.

For Christian Unity

Lord,
we have been praying
for Christian unity
for so long . . .
Will we ever see it?

You came to achieve unity
so long ago . . .
And what are we doing?

It is still time
to bring this unity about,
provided we understand
that the season of the cross
is not a fruitless one . . .

Draw us together, Lord,
you who ceaselessly reconcile us
with the Father
in the Spirit
for ever and ever.

For the Jewish People

Lord Jesus, you were born a Jew
and you died a Jew:
"Jesus the Nazarene, King of the Jews."

The Jews, of course, put you to death.
But what about the Romans?
And what about ourselves?
What a sorry business—
searching for scapegoats
to bear the burden of guilt . . .

Lord,
deliver us from all hatred,
from all racism,
however disguised or unconscious . . .
Grant that someday,
through the risen Christ,
we may come to see
that we are all one nation:
"neither Jews nor Greeks,
neither slaves nor masters,"
but only the children
of one same Father . . .

63

For Those Who Do Not Yet Believe in Jesus Christ

Lord Jesus,
"this is eternal life:
knowing you,
the one true God."

To us who think we believe,
grant a humble faith . . .
And in all men of good will
who seek you,
teach us to recognize
men in whom you believe.

"By His Cross..."

Father most holy,
it is indeed good to offer you thanks
now, when you invite us to relive
what your own Son once lived for us.

In giving up his life on the cross,
he calls us, too,
to offer our lives each day.

In rising from the dead,
he shows us
that no one can take man's life away,
since you are the one who gives it . . .

That is why—
in communion with all the saints,
who share the life
of the risen Christ—
we proclaim
as with one voice:
Holy, holy, holy . . .

● Preface during Lent.

Yes, Father,
it is truly right and just
for us to thank you always,
but especially during these services
where we celebrate the glory
of Christ's cross—
the cross that bathes his resurrection
in all its dazzling light;
the cross that reveals the meaning
of our hope;
the cross that brings reconciliation
for us all.

That is why the entire universe,
saved by the passion of your Son,
constantly recalls
those hours on the cross . . .
That is why your people all know
what glory they are celebrating
when they honor the cross . . .

All of us, then, proclaim
in unison:
Holy, holy, holy . . .

● Preface during Passiontide.

And His Resurrection...

Christ Jesus is here—
here,
as on the first day;
here among us eternally,
as on Easter morning;
here with us for ever
as fully as on the first day;
here in our midst
through all the days of his eternity:
for he is risen!
Alleluia!

● Greeting on Easter Sunday.

Just what did John see
when he went into your tomb, O Lord?
The gospels do not tell, but only say,
"He saw and he believed."
How admirable!
We praise you, Christ Jesus,
for your love is eternal.

When, in times of bitter grief,
we hide to weep alone,
there comes a blinding light.
It is only the certitude
of things we hope for,
but what a certitude!
You are risen, Lord Jesus,
for your love is eternal.

At what moment of that night
between the sabbath
and the first day of the week
did you rise from the dead?
How many dark nights we must endure
to know what dawn is like!
The joy of the resurrection is difficult
and demanding,
for your love is eternal.

● Litanic prayer at the Kyrie on Easter Sunday.

What a lesson you teach us,
Peter and John,
as you run to meet the risen Christ!

When, perhaps,
our faith runs out of breath,
help us,
O Lord,
not to give up . . .
You are here, always here,
and you go before us
as in Galilee . . .
You are risen,
today
and for all eternity.

• Opening prayer on Easter Sunday.

We admire you,
O risen Lord.
That is our way of adoring you.

Renew in us
your own capacity for admiration,
for you admire your very self in us.
And well you may!
Are you not God?

Indeed, you are the Lord,
and you live your resurrection
in each of us
today and every day
for ever and ever.
Amen.

Lord Jesus,
your Eucharist
is the Real Presence
of your resurrection
in the reality of our lives.
And our brotherly communion
with you
is the power of your resurrection
today.

Give us the vigor
to live like new creatures,
not putting off till tomorrow
what we can do today,
and not waiting for the life to come.

How good it is,
Father most holy,
to let our hearts proclaim your glory
on this resplendent night [day]
when Christ, our Love, arose.

What light,
to see the mystery of your life
become the mystery of ours!
What serenity,
to be able to look upon death
as the door to a wholly different life!
What joy,
to be able to share,
with the whole nation of the baptized,
the same faith and the same hope!
What a call, too,
for everyone on earth! . . .

That is why,
in communion with all of creation,
as the new fire crackles with gladness,
we sing in unison:
Holy, holy, holy . . .

● Preface for Easter.

Brothers and sisters,
arise! . . .
If you believe,
then everything is possible . . .

Jesus Christ is risen!
And, already, we are risen with him.

From this moment on,
it depends entirely on us
to let what is impossible
for us
become possible
through Christ.

• Greeting on a Sunday during Eastertide.

Father all good,
in admiration
at what is unique
in the resurrection of your only Son,
we wish we could improvise
ever new refrains.

But how can we express
the inexpressible joy
your Spirit inspires in us?

Like stammering children,
our hearts simply take up the cry
of your entire people:
Alleluia!
He is risen—
he whom you love as yourself,
in the same Spirit,
world without end . . .

Are You
the One My Heart
Is Searching For?

With Great Yearning

Triune God,
you are not
a mathematical proposition . . .

Just as the waves of the sea
hold constant parley
with the sands on the beach,
so shall I keep the eternal yearning
ever rumbling in my heart.

You are the one
my heart is searching for—
you, the one God:
Father-Son-Spirit . . .
Singular plural . . .
for ever and ever!

• Prayer at the General Intercessions on Trinity Sunday.

The horizon is still quite dark,
but hope is about to dawn.
The seed of salvation is sprouting,
as earth makes ready.
What about the roots of our hearts? . . .

(a *moment of silence*)

Just as the sick
throughout the sleepless night
await the dawn,
so we seek your presence, Lord,
amid the fever of these our times.

(a *moment of silence*)

A period of waiting,
waiting for the one we love . . .
What joy!
The season of yearning . . .

(a *moment of silence*)

● Litanic prayer at the Kyrie on the first two Sundays of
Advent.

Lord,
what do we expect of you?
And what do you expect of us?
Forgive us for not waiting
for what you want for us.

(a moment of silence)

Lord,
mankind does not wait for you
in order to be happy,
but eagerly pursues happiness
according to its own lights.
Forgive us for not waiting
for what you want for us.

(a moment of silence)

Lord,
you are near,
and the Church is always waiting.
She thereby manifests
the hope of salvation.
Forgive us for not waiting
for what you want for us.

(a moment of silence)

• Litanic prayer at the Kyrie on the last two Sundays of Advent.

Whom are we waiting for?
Christ Jesus?

Then, what do we expect?
The blind still cannot see,
the lame do not walk any better,
and the prisons are full.
And yet, Christ has come.

The miracle, then, rests with us:
we have to make the light luminous,
the equilibrium equitable,
and justice just . . .
We must not delay.

Like little children,
let us allow the Lord to come to us.
He expects of us
what we expect of him . . .

● Greeting during Advent.

Every time we celebrate the Eucharist
in memory of you, O Lord,
you are present in our midst.

We thank you for enabling us,
whenever we wish,
to share in the sign of your presence
as we await your coming in glory.

● Prayer after communion on the Last Sundays of the year
  which precede Advent.

"If only you knew the gift of God . . ."
It was given so long ago!
And yet, after so many revelations,
what do we desire from him?

"Give me a drink . . ."
We thirst for love.
That is what we say,
but to what source do we go?

"Whoever drinks the water I shall give
will never thirst again . . ."
Is it true we no longer thirst?
Though fed, are we filled? . . .

● Litanic prayer at the Kyrie on a Sunday in Lent when the gospel about the Samaritan woman (John 4, 1-42) is proclaimed.

Each of us carries a desert within,
to be crossed in dryness of faith . . .

Lord,
help us find the well
where you await us
at every stage of our lives.
And we shall set out again,
thirsting, at last,
for none but the living water
which you have promised us.

• Opening prayer on a Sunday in Lent when the gospel
  about the Samaritan woman (John 4, 1-42) is proclaimed.

Father, source of all light,
man would not be man
unless he desired to know everything . . .
And you would not be God
unless you were the one who can.

In Christ Jesus—
God become man—
make each of us yearn
to find you fully
through what we learn of you.
But that will take time—
a lifetime,
not to mention time without end
in the life to come . . .

- Prayer at the General Intercessions on a Sunday in
  Lent when the gospel about the Samaritan woman
  (John 4, 1-42) is proclaimed.

May this Eucharist
intensify our hunger
to know you better,
till the day we live
in the perfect knowledge
of love,
for ever and ever.
Amen.

• Prayer after communion on a Sunday in Lent when the
  gospel about the Samaritan woman (John 4, 1-42) is
  proclaimed.

Seeing, Touching
and Believing

"Do not let your hearts
be troubled."
Do not let them
be roiled
by the turbulence of the times.

But, rather, let them
be stirred
by him alone who can clarify them;
by him who said,
"Happy are those whose hearts are pure,
for they can see
what many do not see."

Like newborn infants, smiling at life,
we discover in you, O Lord,
what true life is.
You are risen.

Like Thomas,
we want to touch you, Lord!
Beyond all proofs,
moved by your love,
we too can say,
"My Lord and my God!"

Like Philip,
we believe that everything is possible
for those who rise with you, O Lord,
this very day.

● Litanic prayer at the Kyrie on a Sunday during Eastertide
(John 14, 1-14).

"Show us the Father,
and we shall be satisfied,"
Philip exclaimed.
Your answer, Lord,
leaves us wanting more.
Yes, show us the Father;
but show us yourself as well,
since we cannot go to him
except through you.

And how, O Lord, can you say,
"To see me is to see the Father"
when you know full well
that we see nothing?
Still, you tell us we know him . . .
But believe us:
we want to believe in you!

Lord, you constantly amaze us.
"Whoever believes in me
will do even greater works
than I perform."
Grant that we may experience
what Paul discovered:
"I can do anything through him
who strengthens me."

● Another litanic prayer at the Kyrie on a Sunday during
Eastertide (John 14, 1-14).

We are not angels, Lord.
As creatures of flesh and blood,
we need to see, to touch, to feel.

You say,
"To see me is to see the Father."
What can that statement mean
to us, today?
We see nothing . . .

But are we listening?
Your word produces no sound,
being the breath of the Spirit.
Create silence, then, in our hearts,
for silence is
the light of the invisible,
and the universal language.

• Opening prayer on a Sunday during Eastertide (John 14,
  1-14).

Lord Jesus,
how we wish
we could touch you,
as Thomas did! . . .
But even in this Eucharist—
while thanking you
for this visible sign
of your invisible presence—
we know full well
that that shall never be . . .
Why, then, should we
still attempt the impossible?

Help us, O Lord, to live
through faith
what you yourself ceaselessly live
in us:
the eternal marvel of your resurrection
for ever and ever . . .

● Prayer after communion on a Sunday during Eastertide
(John 14, 1-14).

If It Is You . . .

Speak to Us:
We Merely Stammer

What a long road has been traveled
since the day the risen Christ
revealed himself
to the disciples from Emmaus!

Yet it is the same road
we walk again today:
Christ is still speaking,
still celebrating the Eucharist.

May his words
and the breaking of the bread,
shared down through the centuries,
renew in us
the fidelity of love
amid the drab realities of life!

● Greeting on a Sunday during Eastertide (Luke 24, 13-35).

"Whatever you ask
in my name
I will do."

We know you keep your word,
O Lord,
and that is why we are troubled
when you seemingly turn a deaf ear
to our cries.

Teach us to ask,
in the fidelity of your Spirit,
what you expect of us.
We merely stammer;
but you, O Lord,
please speak to us.

● Opening prayer on a Sunday during Eastertide (John 14, 12-14).

For centuries now,
O Lord,
we have been hearing people speak
about you,
yet we still do not know how to speak
with you.

But there are so many days
when your words break in our hearts
like an echo that dies . . .
and so many days
when we search for you
as in a dream . . .

Do you remember Samuel?
Then, speak again, O Lord,
"for your servant is listening . . ."
You are the word;
you are silence.

● Prayer at the General Intercessions on a Sunday during
the year (1 Samuel 3, 1-21).

Do Not Forsake Us:
We Are Alone

Lord Jesus,
everyone is at the end of his rope,
everyone is disillusioned . . .
But who or what, O Lord,
can separate us from you?

When we are tempted to forsake you,
grant that we not let ourselves
be engulfed by the shadows
along the road.
For once, make us feel something:
feel that you are holding tight;
for, in your Spirit,
you are our life at the center of life
here and now and for ever.
Amen.

● Opening prayer on a Sunday during the year (Romans 8, 35-39).

Lord Jesus,
at some time or other,
sooner or later,
each of us discovers
in his own life
that night is drawing near . . .

Now, while the light of earth
is dimming for some
and glowing with promise for others,
we give you thanks in this Eucharist
for your life, beyond time,
and your presence at every moment.

But, even so, let us repeat
today,
as to a friend we wish to detain,
"Stay with us, Lord, until the end . . .
for ever and ever!"
Amen.

● Prayer after communion on a Sunday during Eastertide
  (Luke 24, 13-35).

Lord, you know how we aspire
to freedom.
But you also know what chains
we weld for ourselves . . .
Forgive us for building
our own prison.

Lord, we judge others
by what we are,
and too often reduce them to being
only what they seem to us . . .
Forgive us for shutting our neighbor
within our narrow prison.

"I was in prison," you tell us, Lord,
"and you visited me . . ."
We would like to make
your words come true;
but when we leave our brothers
in their loneliness,
it is you yourself we leave in prison.

● Another litanic prayer at the Kyrie on a Sunday in
Advent (Matthew 11, 1-15).

Lord Jesus,
we have not learned to wait.
We want signs and proofs—
right now.
Doubt torments us . . .

Where are you, Lord?
Where should we seek you?
You tell us that the desert is the place
for both solitude and encounters . . .

Make us experience this
in serenity.
That we may welcome our brothers
all the better,
teach us to recollect ourselves in you,
who live in perfect communion
with the Father and the Spirit
for ever and ever.
Amen.

• Opening prayer on a Sunday in Advent (Matthew 11,
1-15).

Lord Jesus,
you alone can reveal to us
the riches of God's solitude
in the communion of Persons.

Alone in the desert
and alone in Gethsemane,
alone on your cross,
between men who were alone on theirs,
you assumed everyone's solitude
within yourself
so that everyone might commune
with God.

O God of encounters,
may each of us
in his desert
detect a sign of your presence.
With you,
may each of us be
for his brothers
a traveling companion
in the fellowship of the Father
and the Spirit.

- Prayer at the General Intercessions on a Sunday in Advent
  (Matthew 11, 1-15).

Lord Jesus,
by taking part
in your death and resurrection,
we pass from solitude to communion.

May this Eucharist,
conquering doubt and fear,
be for everyone
a sign of your passage in our lives,
as we wait for you
in order to live
today.

● Prayer after communion on a Sunday in Advent (Matthew
11, 1-15).

Guide Us
and Strengthen Us

"Seek, and you will find . . ."

Brothers and sisters,
do not let yourselves be stopped
by obstacles along the way.
Christ beckons us on:
he is the shepherd.
He welcomes
and strengthens us:
he is the gate.

● Greeting on a Sunday during Eastertide (John 10, 1-10).

Lord,
you bid us enter into your kingdom.
You are the gate.
Counting on your word,
we come and knock.

Narrow is the portal of the kingdom,
and great the demands of love.
Vast is your heart,
and infinite your tenderness.
We come to seek you, Lord.

You are truly our shepherd,
as we often sing:
"The Lord is my shepherd,
nothing shall I want."
May this assurance spur us on,
with unshakeable faith.
Our search for you, O Lord,
will never end.

● Litanic prayer at the Kyrie on a Sunday during Eastertide (John 10, 1-10).

Lord, you are not a God
who reassures us readily.
But, like an Alpine guide,
you help us stand firm . . .
for you are Love.
Strengthen us in that love.

Lord, when adverse winds churn the sea
and night doubles our terror,
may your cry come across to us:
"Courage! It is I: do not fear."

Lord, to each of us
you say, "Come."
Speak up a little louder . . .
Command us to go to you.

• Litanic prayer at the Kyrie on a Sunday during the year
  (Matthew 14, 22-23).

Lord Jesus,
just what do you mean
when you call yourself
our shepherd?
You guide us, of course,
and call us . . .
But who has ever heard
the sound of your voice?

It is in the silence of faith
that you speak . . .
and in the silence
of the hidden things of life
that we must reply . . .

Then, grant that we may find
in the Gospel today,
not mere words,
but your life-giving words,
for you are the Word of God.

• Opening prayer on a Sunday during Eastertide (John 10,
1-10).

Lord Jesus,
you bid us follow you . . .

But we are not sheep.
We desire
not only to walk behind you
but to catch up with your love,
which outruns us . . .

And since you reveal yourself
as the one who draws us on,
may we believe
in the progress you help us make.

● Prayer at the General Intercessions on a Sunday during Eastertide (John 10, 1-10).

106

Once again
you have spoken to us;
once again
you have given us your bread.

You are always the same for us,
who are so different.
You alone,
the true and good shepherd,
can bring about communion
between us
and all who do not know your fold.

As you promised once,
enable us "to go in and out"
so as to share the joy of your love
with everyone
in the freedom of the children of God.

● Prayer after communion on a Sunday during Eastertide
(John 10, 1-10).

Forgive Us
and Save Us

A CRY FOR HELP

Renew, O Lord,
the gift of yourself in me.
I have seen too much,
am not growing old very gracefully,
and have not learned how to suffer.

Like snow,
may bitterness melt from me!
Like the sun,
may wisdom rise within me!
May rebellion burn itself out,
while fervor burns always brighter!

Do not harden my mind, O Lord,
but simplify my heart.
Over the years,
what beautiful things
I have forgotten or scorned
in the name of sophistication . . .

Mary, born without sin,
be a living presence to us;
for we need to know
that someone from our midst—
oh, the matchless woman!—
never squandered a single gift.

But as for us,

forgive us, Lord:
we enjoy no special favor
and can do nothing about it.

Violence and torture,
hatred and war,
debauchery and vice,
misery and hunger,
falsehood and calumny,
vanity and jealousy,
indifference and neglect,
malice and injustice—
these are the works of man.

Love us, Lord:
we are your victory.
Save us,
you who raise us from death!

● Prayer before receiving the sacrament of penance.

WHY, O LORD?

Love me, Lord . . .
What have you made me?
And what have I made you?

I do what you have branded as wrong.
Incurable of myself,
I am sick with sin;
but heal me, and I shall be healed.
Immured within myself,
I am a prisoner of sin;
but free me, and I shall be freed.

Who shall say what is normal
and what is not?
Where are the norms, O Lord,
that you have established for me?
Instead of doing the good I love,
I do the evil I hate,
and no longer have the will
to want what I want . . .
It is no longer I who live,
but sin that lives in me.
Who shall say that this or that
is not natural,
since it is in my nature
to do what I detest
and fail to do what I desire?

Who has subjected me to temptation?
And what is the purpose of it all?
Why must I sound the very bottom
of nothingness?
Why experience that?

Why this scorching lucidity
and this incandescent destruction?
Why be responsible and not responsible
at one and the same time?
So many shadows crisscross the light . . .

Do not drive me to despair, O Lord;
but save me, and I shall be saved.

• Prayer before receiving the sacrament of penance.

PRAYER OF THANKSGIVING

Lord Jesus,
we cannot do anything
without you;
and you yourself
cannot act in us
without our cooperation.

We thank you
for being able to do so much;
but, at the same time,
we see our basic inability
to live up to the fulness of your love.

Save us!
Make us welcome your salvation,
not as a chance to better our lives,
but as the only source of freedom,
without which we cannot break
every last bond
that keeps us enslaved
to ourselves.

• Prayer before receiving the sacrament of penance.

GREETING

Brother, sister,
what have you come to find
in this church?
What are you doing here today [tonight]?
Are you ready to live by the truth?

Do not confuse
a feeling of shame with sin,
the offense with guilt,
remorse with repentance . . .
Be reconciled with yourself:
forgive your very self,
and let joy return . . .

Christ Jesus will save you.
Long ago
Adam and Jesus met:
sin is stronger than man,
but Jesus is stronger than sin.

The paradise man lost
has become the kingdom . . .
It is coming.
It is close by.
It is here . . .

● A penitential service.

ANOTHER GREETING

Brother, sister,
hope stirs in you
like the breath of love.

Do not allow this secret force
to decay,
for it comes from God.

Without it,
you could never welcome his forgiveness;
but, with it,
you will be reconciled with yourself
and find yourself renewed,
rejuvenated,
in the midst of this community.

• A penitential service.

LITANIC PRAYER OF
THANKSGIVING AND PETITION

Our Father in heaven,
may your name be held holy,
may your love be made manifest,
and someday may all men
be able to sing:
"How good is our God!"

We are human, O Lord;
so forgive us
for not predisposing
our souls to prayer,
for being stingy with our time
and avoiding recollection.
Yet how can we help
dispersing ourselves?
Please teach us how . . .
We are human, O Lord:
forgive us.

Our Father in heaven,
may your kingdom be established in us,
may your love become a reality,
and someday may all men
be able to sing:
"How good is our God!"

We are human, O Lord;
so forgive us
for dimming the light of the Gospel
through our cowardice
and our compromises with the world . . .
Forgive our passivity in the State
and our inertia in the Church.

And in our families,
forgive those mutual misunderstandings
and reciprocal wrongs
between husband and wife,
between parents and children,
and between the children themselves . . .
We are human, O Lord:
forgive us.

Our Father in heaven,
may your will be done.
Starting now,
here on earth,
set us firmly in your friendship,
and someday may all men
be able to sing:
"How good is our God!"

Forgive us, Lord, for thwarting—
by stubbornness and infidelity—
the loving plan you have for us.
Forgive us for not trying to learn
what you expect of us.
But how can we know your will
for each of us?
Please make it clear . . .
We are human, O Lord:
forgive us.

Our Father in heaven,
you never fail us,
but always give everyone
the bread of your love.
O God, how good you are!

Forgive us, Lord,

our lack of love,
our discourtesy,
our impatience,
our ready-made judgments,
our indifference
and everything that kills love in us.
We are human, O Lord:
forgive us.

Our Father in heaven,
your love is stronger
than our lack of love.
It is infinity
confined in our limitations.
You more than give: you forgive.
O God, how good you are!

Forgive us, Lord,
for not being able to forgive,
for refusing to be reconciled
with ourselves
and others.
When shall we learn to love
as you love us?
When shall we learn to love others
for themselves—
for your sake—
as you love them?
Forgive us whatever impurity
clouds our gaze.
We are human, O Lord:
forgive us.

Our Father in heaven,
you never crush those who fall.
Do not subject us to temptation,
but make us free to do what is right.
O God, how good you are!

Forgive us, Lord,
for having too often chosen
to travel the slippery slopes . . .
Forgive us for taking all those steps
which sooner or later
lead to the last—
that final step
which hurls us down, headlong . . .
Forgive us for not drawing back
from the brink . . .
Forgive us for letting ourselves drift
into sin . . .
We are children, O Lord—
men and women, perhaps,
but still overgrown children . . .
Lord, forgive us.

CLOSING PRAYER

Lord,
everything is forever starting over:
our sins, our stupidity . . .
But so is your love . . .

When we acknowledge our sins,
we also acknowledge your forgiveness.
Nothing is lost.
Everything starts afresh.

This is hope—
in you, Christ Jesus,
who are with us
all the days of our lives.
Amen.

Our Father in heaven,
holy be your name,
your kingdom come,
your will be done
on earth as in heaven.
Give us today our daily bread.
Forgive us our sins
as we forgive those who sin against us.
Do not subject us to temptation,
but deliver us from evil.

Free us from a crippling
sense of disgrace
and grant us strength
to make a fresh start.
Free us from remorse
and grant us true repentance.

At the request
of the Virgin Mary,
who remained faithful;
of Peter,
who returned to you;
of Paul,
who was converted;
and of so many saints
who were so often forgiven,
let *your peace* shine forth,
O Lord,
and make us want that peace
with all our hearts . . .

One Another

Each Day, an Eternity of Love

When they saw you weeping
by Lazarus' tomb, O Lord,
the Jews said of you,
"See how Jesus loved him!"

When they saw
the early Christian communities,
witnesses said of your followers,
"See how they love one another!"

Hasten the day when,
on seeing your Church,
everyone will say of her,
"See how she loves us!"

● Litanic prayer at the Kyrie on a Sunday in Lent (John 11, 1-44).

Lord,
you have left us
one single commandment.
And you know what
your followers do about it . . .
Yet what a revolution
it could produce! . . .

"Love one another
as I have loved you."

Make us rediscover the newness
of your new commandment,
and help us live
by this eternity of love . . .
each day!

● Opening prayer on a Sunday during the year, or on Holy
  Thursday (John 13 *in toto*).

124

Lord,
just as we sometimes keep humming
our favorite song,
so, too, this morning
we let the eternal refrain of your love
resound in our hearts:
"Love one another as I have loved you."
Oh! the song
of endless ages past and yet to come . . .

- Prayer at the General Intercessions on a Sunday during the year, or on Holy Thursday (John 13 *in toto*).

Lord,
you know the problems we face
trying to live in fellowship.
Whenever two or three unite
to work or dwell together,
clashes and blunders inevitably occur.

May this fraternal Eucharist
re-create
calm for those who are tense
and agreement for those
who no longer agree . . .
And may every home
open its doors this day
to serenity.

• Prayer after communion on a Sunday during the year
  (Matthew 18, 19-20).

126

Our Daily Bread

The bread of men,
the bread of God,
the same bread . . .

The coarse bread of suffering,
the tender bread of love,
the same bread . . .

The bread of every morning,
the bread of every Mass . . .

• Greeting on a Sunday in Lent when the homily is about
the hunger in the world.

127

Bread from the baker
who works at the crack of dawn;
bread with the family
that we join at the end of the day . . .
Man's bread.

Fresh bread of joy,
dry bread of humiliation,
dark bread of suffering,
bread that is lacking . . .
Why must man's bread
become the bread of tears?

Daily bread,
bread of life,
bread of love . . .
God's bread.

• Litanic prayer at the Kyrie on a Sunday in Lent when
  the homily is about the hunger in the world.

Be blessed, O Lord:
you shape us in your love.
Be our yeast
in the dough,
the dough of every day . . .

Be blessed, O Lord:
you sow and you reap.
Ripen the harvest of life
in the sunshine of your love,
the love of every day . . .

Be blessed, O Lord:
you have seen seed fall into the soil;
you have watched wheat spring up;
you have rubbed ears of grain
between your hands;
you know the taste of bread,
the bread of every day . . .

• Litanic prayer at the Kyrie on the solemnity of the Body
  and Blood of Christ.

Father all good,
like the seed which dies in the ground
and bears much fruit,
your Son was crushed by death
so that life might bloom.

As we celebrate
the Bread of life
in the person of your Son Jesus Christ,
triple our capacity to love.
Then we may have enough imagination
to find more and better ways
of sharing our goods with the neediest
and uprooting in ourselves
whatever prevents us
from living with you,
in fellowship with all men
in the oneness of the Son
and the Spirit.

• Opening prayer on a Sunday in Lent when the homily
  is about the hunger in the world.

Father all good,
you give everyone what he needs,
you fail no one,
you let no one down.

If there is a shortage
of bread on earth,
that is because we fall short
of your love . . .

Help us believe
in the infinite value of our smallest acts,
and multiply in the world
the love which you live through us.

- Prayer at the General Intercessions on a Sunday in Lent
  when the homily is about the hunger in the world.

131

Lord Jesus,
the days and the nights
follow one another
perpetually.

With you,
nothing ever ends,
but all is just beginning—
constantly . . .

You are here
to give us the bread of fidelity
every day,
unfailingly.

Accessible God,
you remain at our disposal,
for which we shall thank you
eternally.

● Prayer at the General Intercessions on the solemnity of
  the Body and Blood of Christ.

Father all good,
with so many people dying of hunger,
may this Eucharist
strengthen our faith in your love!

Yes, Lord, we admit it:
from losing hope
in those who have too much of everything,
we could lose hope even in you!

Once again
may this communion be for us
a call to share what we have;
then we can ask you,
without feeling guilty,
"Give us today our daily bread."

● Prayer after communion on a Sunday when the homily
is about the hunger in the world.

Father all good,
our destinies are in your hands,
but we must regulate
our everyday living.

Lord Jesus,
you invite us to share your Eucharist,
but we must invite the world
to share your joy.

Holy Spirit,
you fashion us according to your love,
but we must learn how to love.

● Litanic prayer at the Kyrie, possibly on the solemnity
of the Body and Blood of Christ.

Lord Jesus,
we feast on your word
and your Eucharist.
Like spoiled children
whose every want is satisfied,
we imagine all is well . . .

But how many of us,
baptized though we are
and claiming to be your followers,
think of you each day?
How, then, do we differ
from the indifferent?

How many of us genuinely yearn
to share with you
the love you share with us?
Why, then, do we so glibly mouth
words like *thanksgiving* and *love?*

Astound us, Lord,
and we shall discover love.
Fill us with your eternal wonder,
and someday we shall learn
how to give back—
to you and our fellowmen—
what you give everyone
every day.

• Opening prayer on the solemnity of the Body and Blood
  of Christ.

Lord Jesus,
we offer you
the bread and wine of our life.
May they become your own life,
and may your love become our love!

In this wondrous exchange,
may your Eucharist
transform our hearts!
Teach us to really commune
with those who suffer most.

But how can we give back
what you alone can give?
When we meet in your name,
you are there with us,
and we can ask you
for the impossible . . .

Through the very limits
set by our weakness,
may the joy
of this peaceful assembly spread,
unseen,
throughout the world.

- Another prayer at the General Intercessions, possibly on
  the solemnity of the Body and Blood of Christ.

Lord Jesus,
the riches of your word
and your Eucharist
stagger the human mind.
We are often quite unaware
of the inexhaustible treasure
you ceaselessly offer us.

Since we are reviving
this ever-new gift
in ourselves today,
we earnestly beg
that the abundance of your blessings
may never blunt
our hunger for your love—
the love you share with everyone,
every day.

- Prayer after communion on the solemnity of the Body
  and Blood of Christ.

137

What a Life!

I Want To Live...

With you, O Lord, life is beautiful.
Happy they who remember this
amid the gloom of so many days
and the glory of certain others
that all make up human existence.

In you, O Lord,
death becomes the gateway to life.
But how shall we rise
from our ashes again?
Happy they who die to themselves
in order to live with you,
shaking off this mortal dust
day by day . . .

For you, O Lord, life and death,
the cross and the resurrection,
are not enigmas . . .
Dying and living
are one single mystery—
yours and ours both:
the paschal mystery . . .

• Litanic prayer at the Kyrie on Ash Wednesday.

"Have I not told you,
'Believe, and you will see'?"
We believe, O Lord,
but we do not see.

"Lazarus, come forth!"
You uttered this cry so loud, O Lord,
that it still resounds today.
But where does your voice come from?

"Whoever believes in me,
even though he dies, will live."
Lord, we believe in you.
We know we shall live for ever.
But we also know
that, someday, we shall die . . .

● Litanic prayer at the Kyrie on a Sunday in Lent (John 11, 1-44).

Lord,
we want to live,
and you promise to make us live.

Thanks for this day's life
and, already, for tomorrow's.
Be blessed
now and always
for ever and ever.

● Opening prayer on a Sunday during the year (Mark 5, 35-43).

Lord Jesus,
no two blades of grass are the same,
no two people quite alike.

Your love is incomparable in each of us.
Grant us the wisdom
not to compare ourselves with others . . .
To everyone, you give
the share of joy he needs
to live from day to day,
but the seeming inequality of your gifts
disturbs us . . .

Make us at least honest enough
not to appropriate to ourselves
the heritage you entrust to us
for the happiness of others . . .
Help us evaluate ourselves correctly.
Why minimize our abilities
and those of others?
Why overrate our talents
and underrate those of others?

Yes, others:
always others . . .
Teach us to live
for others.

● Opening prayer on a Sunday during the year (Matthew
25, 14-30).

Lord Jesus,
we celebrate your resurrection
and proclaim:
"You are our life, our God!"

But do you think that, for all that,
we have no questions?
"Why live?" for instance;
"Was I born for this—or for that?"
Like children puzzling over matters
which lie beyond them,
we always want an explanation.
But that is not why you came on earth.

Living—
this is your revelation.
Today, then,
we do not ask you "Why?"
but only "How?":
"How live with you?"

● Prayer at the General Intercessions on a Sunday during the year (John 5, 19-40 and 14, 6-19).

Lord Jesus,
we need to be happy.
So we beg a few crumbs of happiness.
Can you not give
the little we ask?
We would so like to hear you say,
"Let it be as you wish!"

Teach us
to love what you love,
to live what you lived
and dare repeat,
"Not my will, but yours!"

● Prayer at the General Intercessions on one of the first
days of Holy Week.

Lord Jesus,
on our bodies as men and women
you bestow a beauty
they would never possess
if you yourself had not had
the most beautiful body
of all the children of men.

Splendor of the Father's glory,
your body is risen.
Imperfect beauty of creation,
our bodies grow old.
Though stamped with your grace,
they bear the marks
of suffering and sin.

May this Eucharist,
the pledge of eternal life,
be for us the ferment of the Spirit
as we await
the resurrection of our bodies
unto life everlasting.

● Prayer after communion on the solemnity of the Body and Blood of Christ.

Is there anyone who does not thirst
for a fuller life?

You make springs of living water
well up within us, Lord,
for the life that never runs dry.
May this Eucharist, then,
where you give your very self,
be a source of joy to us . . .

It must, O Lord! . . .
How else do you expect us to live
day after day
unless each day contains
at least one drop of joy?

● Another prayer after communion on a Sunday in Lent
  (John 4, 1-24).

On Vacation

"Come to me,
all you who work hard
and bear a heavy burden,
and I will give you rest . . ."

Rest is not necessarily quietude
but, rather, the certitude
of being firmly founded on God,
come what may . . .

May this vacation season,
like an island
in the middle of the year,
prompt us to seek the Lord,
our rock and our strength . . .

● Greeting on a Sunday during the summer.

Lord, it is good to be alive.
We want to live.
But the time is short . . .
like on vacation . . .

Lord, it is good to love.
When we love,
it is always a happy time . . .
like on vacation . . .

Lord, it is good to pray;
but how can we speak to you?
We must find time, take time . . .
like on vacation . . .

● Litanic prayer at the Kyrie on a Sunday during the
summer.

When, O Lord,
shall we ever understand
that praying to you
means speaking with you about love?
When shall we be filled with joy
at the mere thought
of spending a moment with you
simply because you are you? . . .

May this vacation time
be a perfect chance
to draw closer to you,
and may we all set our hearts
on re-balancing ourselves in you,
who live in a harmony
established for all eternity.

• Opening prayer on a Sunday during the summer.

Lord Jesus,
you know our regular routine,
the way we pant and puff
to get everything done,
the crushing weight of days
that are too filled—
or perhaps too empty.

This is vacation time . . .
May our joy
find full measure
in you!

• Prayer at the General Intercessions on a Sunday during
  the summer.

152

Lord,
you give us your love
under the poor and lowly symbol
of bread.

In your Eucharist,
our limitations become yours,
just as your greatness becomes ours.

May the communion
of our weakness with your strength
vivify the words you speak to us
at this vacation season:
"Come to me,
all you who work hard
and bear a heavy burden,
and I will give you rest . . ."

• Prayer after communion on a Sunday during the summer.

153

On Earth . . .

Peace and Unity

Sow the seeds of peace,
all you men of good will!
It is time.
It is still time.
It is Christmas time,
when the Sun rises, eternal . . .
Our mission must be
to carry on this age-old task
unceasingly . . .

● Greeting on the third Sunday in Advent.

Lord, you say, "I want only peace."
Everybody can say the same!
In each war, on both sides,
everyone wants peace—
in his own way . . .
Forgive us for not wanting peace
the way you want it.

Lord, you say, "I leave you my peace."
But what do we do with it?
The folly of war erupts everywhere.
Though we talk of nothing but peace,
we do not know how to live in peace.
Leave us your peace, O Lord;
do not forsake us.

Lord, you say, "I give you my peace."
You bequeathed it to us
once and for all;
and now you offer it to us each day,
always giving and forgiving,
never deserting us.
Forgive us for failing to give peace
as you give it.

• Litanic prayer at the Kyrie on the third Sunday in
Advent.

158

"The Prince of Peace is coming . . ."
Lord Jesus,
that is you—today!
Will we recognize you?

People are uneasy,
and our hearts are troubled.

Help us speak the words of peace
and perform the gestures
of reconciliation that the world needs
in order to live in peace,
without waiting for it to be eternal,
for ever and ever.
Amen.

● Prayer at the General Intercessions on the third Sunday in Advent.

Lord Jesus,
every Eucharist
is a reconciliation.

May this communion of peace
be for all of us today
an urgent call
to seek a gesture of forgiveness,
step by step,
again and again,
for the peace
of countless ages to come . . .
Amen.

"Peace be with you!"
"I give you peace, my peace;
I leave it to you."

Do you not hear Christ repeating today,
like an echo,
"I give you unity, my unity;
I leave it to you . . . to bring about"?

● Greeting at the Mass for Unity.

Father all good, be blessed.
How beautiful your unity is
in the fellowship of Son and Spirit!
How desirable unity is for us
in the assembly of the baptized!
Father all good,
forgive us
for not acknowledging our brothers,
for not pooling our peculiar riches
but always wanting to distinguish
"mine" from "thine" . . .

Lord Jesus, be blessed.
In your eternal love,
you have realized unity.
In your love today, you reveal to us
that it is possible.
May your truth be our truth,
your light, our light!
Lord Jesus,
forgive us
for justifying our inadequacies
by calling darkness light,
evil good,
and falsehood truth.

Spirit of unity, be blessed.
You gather us together from all sides,
and our scattered communities
form a single body in you,
though not yet visibly a single Church.
While hopefully awaiting this joy,
we praise you, we bless and adore you.
Spirit of unity,
forgive us for harboring
old grudges and grievances
in the bosom of our communities

and thus tainting
all communities as a whole
with our own infidelities.

● Litanic prayer of thanksgiving and supplication at the Mass for Unity.

Lord,
one spark does not light a furnace,
nor does one gesture achieve unity.
And yet
there is need of that spark, that flame;
need of that gesture,
that word, that act . . .

Since the spectacular fades so fast
in the mind of man,
make us live your passion for unity
in hidden faithfulness . . .

● Opening prayer at the Mass for Unity.

Lord Jesus,
your Eucharist
reminds us of the price of unity:
you gave your life for it.
How precious it is, then . . .

Help us now
to live our lives as testimony
to the truth of your words:
"I have come to gather in unity
the scattered children of God."
Let it still be so today
and for all times!

● Prayer after communion at the Mass for Unity.

Light

Have you ever hunted out the stars?
The light of night can be seen
only by those who train their eyes.

Lift your heads:
the light comes from on high;
but do not be haughty.
Look about you:
the light shines all around;
but do not disperse yourselves.
Return to the source,
and—as you will see—
God manifests himself.

● Greeting on the solemnity of the Epiphany.

Lord, your light has dawned.
But look:
earth lies in darkness,
and hearts in shadow . . .
Illuminate our hearts, O Lord.

Lord, your light is rising.
But in our dimness what do we see?
Pallid glances, muted eyes . . .
Illuminate our hearts, O Lord.

Lord, someday your light
will rise eternal.
From day to day, guide us
till the day
of your worldwide epiphany.
Illuminate our hearts, O Lord.

● Litanic prayer at the Kyrie on the solemnity of the
Epiphany.

Lord,
we no longer offer you
gold or myrrh . . .
but, now and then,
a bit of incense yet . . .

Through the poverty of our symbols,
we want to express our yearning
to know you
in the total light
of the glory you reveal to us—
not the one this world imagines,
but the glory you bring forth in us
day by day
till finally "the hour has come"
to see you as you see us
for ever and ever.

- Prayer at the General Intercessions on the solemnity of
  the Epiphany.

Lord Jesus,
do not the wise men coming to the crib
portray the slow progress of mankind
called to recognize in you
"the one who saves"?

By the bonds of charity it weaves,
may this Eucharist somehow be
for everyone
with whom we come in daily contact
a sign of salvation,
in this light
which you still reveal to us today
but which has such trouble
shining through
in the sky of our lives . . .

● Prayer after communion on the solemnity of the Epiphany.

Freedom

Lord,
you tell us,
as if it were a matter of course,
"Do not live in the flesh,
but on the spiritual level,
since God's Spirit dwells in you."

That is easy for you to say,
but more difficult for us to live . . .
We inhale the atmosphere of this earth;
we are bound up in this world
like children
in tight-fitting clothes . . .
and we do not know how
to break free any more.

Grant us freedom
as the most marvelous gift
of your love . . .

• Opening prayer on a Sunday during the year (Romans 8,
  1-12).

Every kind of soil in your parable,
O Lord,
is found in our hearts.

Superficial,
caught up in the cares of the day
and attached to trifles,
we give way to futility;
and yet,
like a tireless sower,
you constantly turn over in our hearts
the good soil that holds
promise of harvest.

Free us, then,
from all that is not ourselves,
from all that is not you;
and we shall finally discover
that fruit perseveringly
produced in freedom
remains . . .

● Opening prayer on a Sunday during the year (Matthew
13, 1-13).

Lord,
just as we sense
in the eyes of those we love
the light they bear within,
so we wish we could read
in the occurrences in our lives
the light you cause to shine.

Purify the eyes
with which we look at everything . . .
Do not let us be dazzled
by the tinsel of life.
And, be we rich or poor,
make us free in regard to money;
for if you are our only treasure,
the choice we make
is for all eternity.

• Opening prayer on a Sunday during the year (Matthew
  6, 24).

Lord,
like good soil that bears fruit,
your Eucharist
bears us in your love.

May it be for us
a seeding of charity
and a sign of the joy
of the children of God,
who live in freedom
even now
while awaiting its fulness
in the world to come.

• Prayer after communion on a Sunday during the year
(Matthew 13, 1-13).

As in Heaven . . .

Mary, Mother of God

Lord Jesus,
all generations proclaim your Mother
blessed.
She has found her happiness
in you.
Forgive us for often seeking ours
elsewhere . . .

Lord Jesus,
you have exalted your Mother.
Since you raise the lowly,
forgive us for humiliating them.

Lord Jesus,
you have worked marvels
for her sake.
And what would she not have done
for you?
Forgive us for not being awestruck
at the thought of her.

● Litanic prayer at the Kyrie on a feast of the Blessed
Virgin Mary.

You are beautiful, O Mary:
beautiful beyond all other women,
for you are the Virgin Mother;
supremely beautiful,
for you are the Mother of God.

After thanking your Son,
all of us together acclaim you:
Greetings, Mary, most favored one!
The Lord is with you.
Blessed are you above all other women,
and blessed is Jesus,
the fruit of your womb.
Holy Mary, Mother of God,
pray for us poor sinners
now and at the hour of our death.
Amen.

● Prayer at the General Intercessions on a feast of the
Blessed Virgin Mary.

Lord Jesus,
in matchless fashion,
you are the perfect Son,
for you have crowned your Mother
"with tenderness and love."

We give you thanks
for making this source of affection
flow out upon the whole Church.
May your Eucharist
strengthen these bonds
you yourself create between us
in your Church.

- Prayer after communion on a feast of the Blessed Virgin Mary.

The Apostles,
Witnesses to Jesus Christ

Where are you going?
What kind of life are you living?
What is it all about?
Do you know that someone else
is leading you where, perhaps,
you had not planned to go?

In this,
you are like Peter,
like Paul,
like all the disciples.

● Greeting on the feast of Saints Peter and Paul.

Lord,
only Peter could have said,
"I will follow you wherever you go."
Do you remember? . . .
If I hear the cock crow,
I shall first recall your faithfulness.

Only Paul could have said,
"It is when I am weak
that I am strong."
What a paradox!
How can it be explained?
If I see people wonder . . .
I shall tell them first
about your faithfulness.

Only one who has loved much can sing,
"When love is all we have . . ."
If everyone around is singing flat,
how shall I do otherwise?
I want to believe
the truth of these words:
"The only happiness is love . . ."
That is your faithfulness.

● Litanic Prayer at the Kyrie on the feast of Saints Peter
  and Paul.

Lord Jesus,
like Peter,
each of us can say,
"You know I love you."

But each of us can also add,
"You know what I am capable of . . ."
Everything:
the best and the worst,
both creating and destroying myself . . .

But what can I do without you?
God of faithfulness,
make me capable of you.

Peter—even Peter—doubted:
his faith faltered,
and he almost sank.

As we are tossed about
in the trough between the waves
and all but engulfed
by the floodtides of life,
reach out your hand to us, O Lord.

• Another opening prayer on the feast of Saints Peter and Paul.

Lord Jesus,
at the height of the storm,
your disciples panicked
and cried out in fear, "It is a ghost!"

As we cross the sea of life,
we are tempted to believe
that you slip past
like a wave.
On this feast of Peter and Paul—
your two inseparables—
strengthen in us
the intrepid faith of the apostles;
and may your Church never shy
from the challenges
of the mission
you entrust to her!

● Prayer at the General Intercessions on the feast of Saints
  Peter and Paul.

184

Lord,
we thank you for being able,
at every Eucharist,
to make our own
the apostles' profession of faith:
"You are the Christ,
the Son of the living God."

You are alive—
so alive
that "it is no longer I who live."

But who am I
and who are you, O Lord,
to live like this
in me,
in others,
in God,
for ever and ever?

● Prayer after communion on the feast of Saints Peter and Paul.

At this Eucharist,
O Lord,
we have just gone to the altar rail,
and you have given us your bread.

Following Peter's example,
we readily declare,
"You are the Son of the living God!"

And yet, down deep in every heart,
there lurks a secret fear.
Why are we so apprehensive
when we have set sail with you
for life—
for ever and ever?

● Another prayer after communion on the feast of Saints
  Peter and Paul.

Through Baptism, We Belong to the Same Family...

"What love the Father
has lavished on us,
calling us children of God!
And it is true:
we are!"

Happy at the thought of it,
let us make our joy visible to all . . .

* Greeting on a Sunday after Epiphany when the feast of Jesus' baptism (Matthew 3, 13-17) is celebrated.

Father all good,
through baptism, you give us
what you gave your only Son:
children filled with love.
Be for ever blessed!

Lord Jesus,
through baptism, it becomes manifest
that we are members of the Family.
You live with us
what you live with the Father
and the Spirit.
Be for ever blessed!

Spirit of God,
through baptism, we make visible
this body which you animate—
your Church, our Church.
Your life becomes our life.
Be for ever blessed!

• Litanic prayer at the Kyrie on a Sunday after Epiphany
  when the feast of Jesus' baptism (Matthew 3, 13-17) is
  celebrated.

Most loving Father,
where is the voice
that came from heaven:
"You are my son, the Beloved,
on whom my favor rests"?
Have its vibrations faded, with time,
from the face of the earth?

But why ask
when we know full well?
At baptism
each of us can hear you say,
like an echo,
"You are the one I love;
in you I hope to recognize my Love."

May we hear your voice, O Lord,
in the silence of fidelity,
through him who, in a unique way,
is your Son in the Spirit
for ever and ever!

• Opening prayer on a Sunday after Epiphany when the
  feast of Jesus' baptism (Matthew 3, 13-17) is celebrated.

Lord Jesus,
most of us were baptized
while still babes in arms.
Before we could even walk or talk,
you proved your confidence in us,
for your love does not wait.
From its very dawning,
you offered us the sign
that we belong to your family
in the affection of the Church.

We thank you
and ask you now to grant us
the wholesome boldness to show,
in word and deed,
what your salvation means today.
Give us courage to set about
making the baptized into a nation
where it is good
for all the nations on earth to live . . .
Then shall we see your salvation!

• Prayer at the General Intercessions on a Sunday after
  Epiphany when the feast of Jesus' baptism (Matthew 3,
  13-17) is celebrated.

190

Lord,
your disciples recognized you
in the breaking of the bread.
Will people today
be able to recognize us
as witnesses to your resurrection
from the way we spread your love about?

May this fraternal Eucharist
draw a life-giving response
from our baptized hearts
today,
tomorrow,
and every day
throughout the ages to come.

● Prayer after communion on a Sunday after Epiphany
when the feast of Jesus' baptism (Matthew 3, 13-17) is
celebrated.

191

Our Father in heaven,
you who see things from above,
tell us what has changed
since the day your Son Jesus Christ
came on earth.
The Gospel has spread to every land,
but what about brotherly love?
The Church is worldwide,
but what are the baptized
doing for the world?
Yes, what are we really achieving?

Make us persistent enough
to keep setting out
in the wake of him
whom you once sent
and who now sends us
into this world which you love . . .

● Opening prayer on Mission Sunday.

An Eternal Dwelling

An Internal Dwelling

Now and at the Hour
of Our Death...

Mary, Mother of Christ,
you transmitted life to your only child.
(You were beautiful . . .
Were you even twenty at the time?)
Then you watched him grow
and become that astonishing Man . . .
till the day you received his death
into your hands.
You had given your life for him,
and he gave his for us . . .

Virgin Mary,
you are like a mother's presence
in the Church—
one whose silence speaks of tenderness.
You can understand our heartache.

Now, at the hour of N——————'s death,
and at the hour of our own,
be a light for us
along the passageway
to eternity.
Amen!

• At a wake, prayer to the Blessed Virgin Mary.

Lord Jesus,
if pity is the badge
of a noble human love
that can no longer do anything,
have pity on us.

Lord Jesus,
if pity becomes faith
in your love,
which can do everything,
have pity on us.

Lord Jesus,
if, amid silent tears,
pity becomes hope,
have pity on us.

● Litanic prayer at the Kyrie.

Over Beyond...

Lord Jesus,
you loved life
as no one has ever loved it,
and you experienced death
as no one has ever experienced it.
We thank you because,
with perfect freedom,
you gave yourself up to death
so that, beyond our death,
your life might be our life.

In our grief
at seeing our beloved N——— go away,
make our love strong enough
to rejoice
in the happiness [s]he is experiencing
for the life
of endless ages to come!

● Prayer at the General Intercessions.

The Last Farewell

Before he comes into the light of day,
every mortal knows
the dark warmth of budding life
in his mother's womb.
The primal mystery . . .

Before [s]he is buried in the shadows,
N———, called to the fulness of Light,
will enter earth's fruitful womb.
Who can penetrate the secrets
of the eternal transformation?
The ultimate mystery . . .

Lord,
because of what you told Nicodemus,
receive the soul of N———,
who by baptism
manifested his [her] desire
to be reborn.
May this coffin remind us
that beyond our familiar dwellings
there is ample room
in the Father's house
for ever and ever.

● Meditation before going to the cemetery.

In This
Twentieth Century

Lord of All Nations

God of the universe,
you are the Lord
of all nations on earth.
You call them each by name
and give them being.

Remember your own race
and all races for ever.
You built your people once
from a handful of men
Abraham gathered under the stars . . .
In each emerging nation today,
raise up leaders
to prepare the paths of salvation . . .
And may the shadow of death be banished!

Hear our prayer, the whole world's cry.
Do not scorn
our meager gains in solidarity,
but help them give rise
to what you call
"men of good will,"
without whom we could never hope
to find the road to peace
in this twentieth century—
our century in the long line
of ages past and yet to come . . .

● Prayer at the General Intercessions for emerging nations
  and the progress of mankind.

"The Word Was Made Flesh..."

God our God, you are God!
Who are you
that man should still remember?
God of mankind,
what are we
that you should care for us?

God become man,
humanize what is still inhuman
and divinize what is not yet divine
in this twentieth century of ours.

"And He Dwelt Among Us..."

Lord Jesus,
from day to day
and moment to moment,
may your dwelling be ours,
so that we may find you
at the center of everything—
alive,
mcre alive than all else that lives,
since you are our life
for ever and ever.
Amen.

● Morning prayer.

From Age to Age

Lord Jesus,
your Mother was like you
and never wavered.

May her fidelity extend
from age to age
to all who fear
they cannot stand fast
till the end . . .
May her loving presence
keep us close to you
in this twentieth century,
our century in the onrolling ages.

● Evening prayer on a feast of the Blessed Virgin Mary.

Prayer for the World

God, our Creator,
how glorious a hymn
earth sings to you!
God, our Savior,
how solemn a Mass
the whole world celebrates!
Spirit of Love,
you have our hearts to love in
and our hands to work with . . .

Consecrate us in your truth.
Then both you and we shall live,
through Jesus Christ,
in this twentieth century—
our moment in the course of the ages.

• Prayer for May 1.

Our Offering

Here is the bread:
the dark bread of sorrow,
the white bread of tenderness:
the bread of man,
the Bread of God.

Here is the wine:
the folly of so many joys squandered,
the delight of so many shared:
the wine of man,
the Wine of God.

• Offertory in troubled times.

Liturgical Index

---

4. EASTERTIDE

5. PENTECOST

6. SUNDAYS DURING THE YEAR

Celebrations

Thematic Index

When several references are given for a word, the numbers in italics indicate the pages where a theme seems to have been treated more explicitly.